COPING WITH SUICIDE

DR DONALD SCOTT is Consultant in Clinical Neurophysiology at the London Hospital. He is the author of several books and over a hundred articles on neurophysiology, epilepsy and psychiatry. His books for a non-professional readership include – *Beating Job Burnout,* also published by Sheldon Press. Dr Scott lives with his wife and two children in Blackheath.

Overcoming Common Problems Series

Overcoming Common Problems Series

Family First Aid and Emergency Handbook
DR ANDREW STANWAY

Feverfew
A traditional herbal remedy for migraine and arthritis
DR STEWART JOHNSON

Fight Your Phobia and Win
DAVID LEWIS

Flying Without Fear
TESSA DUCKWORTH AND DAVID MILLER

Goodbye Backache
DR DAVID IMRIE WITH COLLEEN DIMSON

Good Publicity Guide
REGINALD PEPLOW

Helping Children Cope with Divorce
ROSEMARY WELLS

Helping Children Cope with Grief
ROSEMARY WELLS

How to Be Your Own Best Friend
DR PAUL HAUCK

How to Control your Drinking
DRS W. MILLER AND R. MUNOZ

How to Cope with Stress
DR PETER TYRER

How to Cope with your Child's Allergies
DR PAUL CARSON

How to Cope with your Nerves
DR TONY LAKE

How to Cope with Tinnitus and Hearing Loss
DR ROBERT YOUNGSON

How to Cure Your Ulcer
ANNE CHARLISH AND DR BRIAN GAZZARD

How to Do What You Want to Do
DR PAUL HAUCK

How to Enjoy Your Old Age
DR B. F. SKINNER AND M. E. VAUGHAN

How to Improve Your Confidence
DR KENNETH HAMBLY

How to Interview and Be Interviewed
MICHELE BROWN AND GYLES BRANDRETH

How to Love a Difficult Man
NANCY GOOD

How to Love and be Loved
DR PAUL HAUCK

How to Make Successful Decisions
ALISON HARDINGHAM

How to Pass Your Driving Test
DONALD RIDLAND

How to Say No to Alcohol
KEITH McNEILL

How to Sleep Better
DR PETER TYRER

How to Stand up for Yourself
DR PAUL HAUCK

How to Start a Conversation and Make Friends
DON GABOR

How to Stop Feeling Guilty
DR VERNON COLEMAN

How to Stop Smoking
GEORGE TARGET

How to Stop Taking Tranquillisers
DR PETER TYRER

Hysterectomy
SUZIE HAYMAN

If Your Child is Diabetic
JOANNE ELLIOTT

Jealousy
DR PAUL HAUCK

Learning to Live with Multiple Sclerosis
DR ROBERT POVEY, ROBIN DOWIE AND GILLIAN PRETT

Overcoming Common Problems Series

Overcoming Common Problems

COPING WITH SUICIDE

Dr Donald Scott

SHELDON PRESS
LONDON

First published in Great Britain 1989
Sheldon Press, SPCK, Marylebone Road, London NW1 4DU

© Donald F. Scott 1989

British Library Cataloguing in Publication Data
Scott, Donald
  Coping with suicide. — (Overcoming common problems)
  1. Suicide
  I. Title   II. Series
  362.2
  ISBN 0–85969–585–9

Typeset by Deltatype Ltd, Ellesmere Port, Cheshire
Printed and bound in Great Britain by Courier International Ltd, Tiptree, Essex

Contents

Acknowledgements

I would like to thank Rita Udall and Helen Young for advice on earlier versions of the manuscript, as well as many other colleagues for helpful suggestions, AMS for help with editing, and Mrs P. Siddall for her persistence in typing various drafts of the book. Finally, thanks are due to Joanna Moriarty and Darley Anderson of Sheldon Press for their encouragement, without which writing this book would not have been possible.

DFS

1

The Size of the Problem

Suicide is commoner than we like to admit. Death in any form is upsetting, but suicide also raises quite another set of disturbing emotions—sadness mixed with anger, grief tinged with irritation. Many questions are asked. Why did it happen? Why didn't he/she ask for help? Why did he/she bring shame on our family? Others crowd into the mind.

In this book we shall examine motives behind self-destruction, show the signs that close relatives, friends or even acquaintances can watch for and what they can do about these; and, if the sad event occurs, how to cope with the mixed feelings that inevitably result.

We shall also see how suicide can be prevented. On the way we shall examine the problems of those who definitely want to die because they are suffering from cancer or a slowly progressive illness, together with the moral and legal issues which this raises, not only for the doctor in whose hands the final act must be, but also for family, friends, priest or social worker, and others who may have decided views.

The word 'suicide' even today gives us a jolt. Still a taboo subject, it is not talked about openly, even within the tight circle of family and friends. Recently more open discussion has come about partly due to increasing interest in euthanasia and the founding of the Voluntary Euthanasia Society (EXIT). The ready availability of information provided on suicide as a means of relieving the suffering of the terminally ill caused much outrage, widespread concern, and court cases concerning legality. Yet as a result many more people are now talking and writing openly about self-destruction.

Suicide is an unpleasant subject. No one can expect it to be otherwise. It is one of the many aspects of life that we would rather not face, but we must. First of all we should attempt to enter the mind of the person thinking about suicide and try to have some idea of the desperation he/she feels. Desperation, I think, is the word that seems to sum up most completely the common factor in all suicides.

The distaste for the subject of suicide has another important effect. Although no longer a criminal offence, it tends to be overlooked as a cause of death, to spare the suffering of the family. Further, if the Coroner is unable to decide whether or not a definite intent to die existed, then a verdict of misadventure may be recorded. A suicide note usually clarifies the matter, although in some cases this evidence may be destroyed by a relative or friend, so doubt may remain as to the real cause of death. If the actual number who die by suicide is not known it is clearly difficult to judge whether preventive measures are having any effect. However, there is no doubt that it is a major cause of death. To put this in perspective, the figures for those who die on the roads are, though higher, not very different, yet suicide attracts far less publicity particularly from the preventive point of view.

For those who try to commit suicide repeatedly the professionals use the term 'attempted suicide'. Clearly the individual must be in a state of serious tension even to think about such an action and to make the effort to carry it out. Unfortunately, when this happens several times, family, friends and helpers become less and less concerned and even disinterested. They come to regard actions as merely irritating attention-seeking ploys. There may well be truth in that view, but sadly perhaps as many as 5 per cent of the 'repeaters' in fact kill themselves in the end.

Four case histories

Here the stories of four quite different people who took action to end their lives are recounted. These will give us some understanding of feelings and problems of the suicides at the time. Throughout the book we shall return to these four, and include other accounts of suicidal behaviour to gain a clearer overall picture.

Jill

As a teenager Jill suffered from epilepsy, asthma and a disfiguring skin rash. She had coped remarkably well with all this until a boyfriend made a derogatory remark. She was deeply hurt. Jill's friends all rallied round but one day she did not appear at school. On returning from work earlier than usual, her mother found her deeply unconscious after an overdose of tablets. Was this a serious suicide attempt or not? Almost certainly it was at the time, but happily fifteen years on she is married and well, with her epilepsy under reasonable control.

Peter

Peter, just 21, was a motor mechanic who enjoyed his work, but found it very difficult to make friends. His elder brother had married and left home. His father had, when younger, been part of the criminal fraternity, and had a serious addiction to both alcohol and tranquillizers. This was Peter's background. On this particular Christmas he felt isolated, and apart from one drinking spree with a friend and an all-night party, he shut himself in his room and watched television. One morning he was found semi-conscious, a bottle of his father's tablets by his side. To the amazement of his parents he was dressed in women's clothes. When he recovered from the overdose in hospital it became clear that he had major emotional and sexual problems. These needed long-term professional help for a happy outcome.

Edward

At the time of his death Edward was 44, a business executive who a few months before had been made redundant. His successful career began early and most of his working life was spent with a large prestigious inter-national company. Everything on the surface was 'fine' yet a close friend confided that he 'knocked' his wife and children about, and during his career had a long period of absence from work with a severe psychiatric illness. A two year stint in Europe was successful, and he returned to the United Kingdom to take a better post. However, redundancy soon followed, and not long after that, suicide. We shall return to the question of work, unemployment and suicide but suffice it to say at this point Edward was a vulnerable person and redundancy was the last straw. He could not cope.

Stewart

Stewart was a successful retired farmer. At first all went well in retirement and he and his wife enjoyed life unencumbered by business concerns; sadly after a long drawn-out decline his wife died. Stewart felt his life had collapsed; he had arthritis, and also needed operations for a urinary complaint. For him suddenly there was nothing. He hanged himself within a few months of his wife's death despite efforts to help him organize a new way of life. It is possible that with the right help and medication (he failed to take any prescribed) he would have survived several more healthy, relatively happy years in spite of arthritis. Sadly it was not to be.

2

What Leads to Suicide?

In an attempt to find out just what may lead to suicide, a number of psychiatrists throughout the world have interviewed relatives, friends and associates of those who killed themselves. The results are important and revealing because so often it is said that those who threaten suicide do not actually do it. In fact the vast majority of suicides had told several relatives, friends or other close contacts such as priests of their intentions many times in the weeks and days that led up to their death. *We must take threats seriously*.

The old and infirm were shown to be at greatest risk, men were at more risk than women, and those who drank large quantities of alcohol compared with those who did not. But there is now a changing tendency in the pattern of suicide and younger people are becoming more likely to kill themselves (see Chapter 5). This is possibly due to many different factors including, for example, drug abuse, and widespread unemployment.

The sex factor

This is dealt with more fully in Chapter 4. Men and women behave quite differently in their attitudes towards self-destruction, a well-recognized fact for many years. In general, men commit suicide while women tend to make gestures and actual death is less frequent. However, the number of men caught up in suicidal behaviour is smaller than women.

Why should there be such differences?

For women, one important factor must be hormonal changes in menstruation, child bearing, and the menopause, for these influence both body and mind. However, this is just one side of the coin. The other is the pressure of bringing up children, running a home and often having a responsible job as well. All contribute. So it is not surprising that there is considerable tension in the lives of many women. Another unsurprising fact is that suicidal behaviour often occurs just before a period when the premenstrual symptoms are at their height. However, this is a complex matter because, for example, women taking the Pill differ in their attitudes to suicide from those using other methods of contraception.

Psychological problems that occur after the birth of a child are, in a minority of women, associated with severe depressive or other clearcut psychiatric illness. These may lead to suicide and sometimes, sadly, to killing of the baby as well. Such a pattern has been known since the beginning of history. A watchful eye is needed at this time, so that any signs of undue anxiety about the baby, or bodily health or a marked mood change, can be dealt with at once.

The menopause is an important factor because then permanent hormonal changes are greater than at any other time of life. At this time there is also a change in attitude in general, and increasing concern about appearance—signs of skin ageing and weight gain are just two physical aspects. These, and other psychological changes are partly related to hormonal changes. Some of these symptoms can be helped by hormone replacement therapy (HRT), but this may cause other fears and worries, probably, though temporary relief of such symptoms as hot flushes can be gained, long-term taking of supplements is inadvisable.

This is dealt with further in Chapter 4.

Serious sexual problems

Some individuals have serious sexual difficulties. The problem of AIDS has already occupied many column inches of space and hours of air time on radio and television, but it should be mentioned as a well-recognized cause of suicidal behaviour. It was clear that Peter (see Chapter 1), found unconscious in female underclothes, had a problem that his parents had not known about. Indeed, they would have probably denied that any problem existed. In this case, acceptance by the family was a step forward to successful integration into the community.

The role of the doctor

Even with apparently hasty acts, after consideration, often warning signs could be found; a long period of rumination about life and its purpose probably occurred before the act. In this context serious physical illness is also important. Here a man or woman sees no escape from its grips, other than death, and this may be brought about prematurely by their own hand. Cancer comes to mind first, but other wasting diseases of body and brain are progressively more and more paralysing in both movement and thought, and far more drawn out than cancer—multiple sclerosis, motor neurone disease and Parkinson's disease, for example.

In such instances some seek the advice of their family doctor or ask him for direct help to escape from their present dreadful life. The role of the doctor is difficult. He may feel he should assist actively but this is clearly against his Hippocratic Oath. Would he be taking, rightly or wrongly, a 'God-like' role in terminating a life? Clearly decisions in this matter are very near the boundary of the doctor's true place in society, to care for the sick. The distinction between prolonging life and *actively* ending it—euthanasia—is very close. Currently this is a matter of fierce discussion: in Holland, for example, some doctors already play an active role in 'mercy killing', as we shall see in Chapter 9.

Death wish

The action of the seriously depressed patient who takes all her tablets at once is easily understood. Here the place of the doctor is in no doubt. Appropriate action can be effective not only at that particular time but as part of a long-term treatment. There is, however, a wider question of the 'death wish', suggested by Freud and other psychoanalysts. Is there a deep innate longing in all of us to die, vying with our will to live? If the equation becomes unbalanced is suicide then inevitable?

3

The Contributory Factors

Definitions

One dictionary meaning of the word 'suicide' is: 'one who kills himself intentionally', and then immediately adds 'self-murder'. This shows at once that there is perhaps surprisingly a link between murder and suicide.

Psychiatrists define 'attempted suicide' as 'one who attempts and fails to kill himself'.

Attempted suicide is an important concept, because it leads understandably to the thought that something that failed might have succeeded by accident rather than by design. The whole question of the motive and intention of a potential suicide has to be explored. The subject is still one of continuing medical and psychological controversy, but it is important at this stage for us to grapple with this notion as it leads to better understanding of the subject.

Professor Stengel's well-known book *Suicide and Attempted Suicide* (1964), as well as many professional articles, made a clear distinction between what at this point (though I hate the wording) is sometimes called 'successful' and 'unsuccessful' suicides. This seems too cold, unemotional and even cynical in the context of death or otherwise towards an individual who should be an integrated part of society. In some cases the gravity of their actions showed that they were clearly aimed at ending life, while at the other end of the scale are so trivial that the person could not really have wanted to die.

For this reason the experts have used a variety of

different words to describe 'attempted suicide', though I prefer to use this term and will do so throughout this book. There are, for example, the phrases 'self-mutilation' and 'self-poisoning', which are self-explanatory, and the unfamiliar 'pseudocide' and 'parasuicide'. But whichever word is used there is no denying that the problem exists when, for example, someone is found unconscious with a bottle of tablets by their bed. What was their intention? Was it really to kill themselves, or just a warning action carried out to gain temporary respite from an intolerable situation?

Very often it turns out that getting a short breathing space, and not to die, was the intention. It is also very difficult to assess whether the dose was taken to produce a long sleep or to end it all. So, often, someone with very serious suicidal intentions remains alive, and a person who apparently had no real desire to die, in fact does kill himself, almost by accident. Another view from the professional angle is to regard attempted suicide as a deed which mimics the act of suicide but does not, for one reason or another, have a fatal outcome.

Attempted suicide: two case histories

Jill

Jill, whom we met in Chapter 1, as a teenager took a massive dose of tablets, which would have been fatal if she had not been discovered by her mother returning from work earlier than usual. As so often in these cases, when she recovered the whole incident was so blurred that it was never clear whether she wanted to die or not. Apparently, many people who take an overdose of tablets do so in the heat of the moment; they consider that their action is safe

11

and that they are likely to be rescued, but sadly this does not always happen.

Cecilia

Cecilia was another teenager who like others of her age group injure themselves in desperation. They may use a pair of blunt scissors on their wrists, but in spite of repeated slashes the skin is barely broken and only a little blood oozes. Some young girls quickly grow out of this habit, but some persist and below is one such case.

Cecilia was only eight years old when she first injured herself deliberately. She stuck a needle into her knee. Quite surprisingly it went into the joint space, the gap between the thigh and calf bones. This is, in fact, quite a difficult feat even for a trained surgeon. She said 'I knelt on it' and she was believed. There followed an operation, days in hospital with caring nurses and doctors, and no questions asked. When Cecilia finally came to a psychiatrist, looking back it was clear that this was the first real sign of serious conflict in the family. Father had left home and mother was coping with Cecilia and her older, cleverer, better-looking sister.

At 16 the next problem arose, although at 13 she had been unconscious for several weeks with a mysterious illness labelled 'encephalitis'; no cause was found. The injury this time was a burn on the hand. It seemed trivial, but as the days and weeks went by it did not heal. The finger joints of the little and index fingers 'seized up' and Cecilia was admitted to hospital again for surgery, with anaesthetic, for manipulation to loosen the joints and apply a skin graft. As the time passed, a series of patients occupied the next bed. One by chance was the same age as Cecilia, and though admitted for appendicitis, she had frequent epileptic fits. Cecilia helped care for the teenager, who soon recovered and went home, but she left a 'shadow'. Cecilia fainted once or twice, then came a fit, followed by more and more violent ones where she always fell forward and frequently banged her forehead. Enormous bruises developed which never dispersed; she looked hideous with her almost constant 'black eyes'. She was diagnosed as in need of psychiatric help and trans-ferred to a psychiatric hospital. There after almost a year of intensive treatment she left the ward of her own accord, and disappeared. A month later I received a phone call. She was unconscious and having constant fits in a nearby hospital. The crisis was resolved with psychiatric help, and after another year of psychotherapy she returned home, only to relapse yet again.

Finally she found satisfaction with a flat of her own and a job in a local pony stable. If her psychological plight had not been recognized, her 'attempted suicides' would almost certainly have led to her early death.

War and suicide

While economic depression appears to cause an increase in suicide, war, most unexpectedly, shows the opposite trend, with a distinct *fall* in suicide.

This has been underlined by consideration of suicide in Northern Ireland over the last twenty years. We might have expected that the IRA terrorist campaign would lead to an increase in depressive illness but quite the reverse has been found. This paradox has been noted in other countries, such as Cyprus, during political unrest. The reason for this appears to lie in the feelings of aggression we all have inside us. As we gain maturity we learn to cope with these feelings and direct them into socially acceptable channels. An obvious example is the physical activity of body contact sports. But other aggressions, like vandalism, are directed at property not people. If these aggressive tendencies are not dealt with they build up inside and become intolerable. This leads to a depressive state and may cause self-directed aggressive attitudes leading to, at worst, suicide. During political turmoil these aggressive tendencies are not sublimated, but expressed directly by violence to property and people, hence the fall in suicide rates in war whether civil or world wide.

Suicide, religion and community

One of the factors operating against suicide is personal contact and life within an organized closeknit community. The country has fewer suicides than the city, and the bigger the city the worse the suicide rate. This is partly due to the drift of those without roots, to large cities, often because of their anonymity. Within these conurbations it is quite understandable why, for example, migrant groups or minority religious communities, cling together for mutual support. Prevention could be achieved by bringing the isolated into personal contact with others, and then welding them into some kind of group—artistic, political, religious, it does not matter what as long as they feel they *belong*.

Loneliness

Social isolation, the 'official' term for loneliness, is sometimes brought about by physical illness in both younger and older individuals, particularly the latter. This may be physical, like the problems created by a wheelchair, chronic neurological disorders such as multiple sclerosis, or the result of a serious accident. A recent striking example was a young policeman rendered chairbound because of injury to his spine caused by an assailant's gunshot wound, which also threatened his virility; he became socially isolated, and committed suicide. In the older person arthritis, perhaps complicated with poor hearing or deterioration of vision produced by cataracts may be a factor. Sufferers sometimes develop strange ideas about noises, interpreting odd tappings as ghost-like phenomena or threatening voices; this leads to serious mental disorders.

Frustration: a key word

The background of many attempted suicides can be summed up in one word: 'frustration'. The aim is not to *end life* but rather to *escape*. It is often a blind, explosive, unplanned answer to an intolerable situation: problems with money, children, physical illness, unemployment— perhaps made worse by poor housing, little opportunity for leisure and relaxation. In the background is perhaps a childhood history of little love or affection, neglect or even physical violence.

These factors are often a feature of inner city life, particularly notable in the East End of London where I work. To make matters worse there is a high proportion of immigrants who have had no previous experience of life in a big city and whose quite natural habits do not conform to the traditional 'East Enders'. This is coupled with high illness rates of all types and in all ages, especially in babies and during early life. There are also many stillbirths.

Parents are often addicted to alcohol; drugs are a feature of teenage life and crimes of all kinds are an everyday occurrence. The causes of attempted suicide are obviously numerous, and in individual cases the motives are extremely mixed, varying from sudden blind reactions in a crisis to more drawn out consideration of apparently insoluble problems.

From a medical standpoint those with clearcut depressive symptoms may respond to short-term drug therapy even though there are many problems causing the illness. But bringing about changes in the background is much more difficult, so not surprisingly attempted suicide is not just an isolated incident. Repeated attempts are inevitably fatal in a small minority of cases.

4

Women, Hormones and Suicide

In both men and women hormones are important not only in shaping the body but also the mind. In women the pattern is more complex because of the fluctuation of hormone levels in the blood which vary during the menstrual cycle and have both physical and psychological effects.

Puberty and menstruation

In both sexes puberty is when individual behaviour is said to be 'difficult' by parents although the mature child sees clearly the boot is on the other foot. 'It is odd how much my parents have learnt,' wisely proclaims the 18-year-old, 'since I was 13.'

The changes in body and behaviour at this age are partly brought about by hormones, the upsurge of the female oestrogen and the male testosterone, although both sexes have small amounts of each opposite hormone. For the teenager life is changing markedly; apart from sexual arousal and obvious alterations in the body there are important changes in experience—making decisions as to subjects they take for GCSE at school, and in personal matters in all areas of life. Girls may have to consider taking the contraceptive pill, with or without parental consent. For some there is also experimentation with drugs and alcohol.

Suicidal behaviour in teenagers is different from those in adults. One example we often see is a copycat element where groups of teenagers become involved together (see Chapter 5).

For the young woman the teenager stage is particularly difficult because periods begin, and dealing with this matter physically often produces difficulties. Suicidal behaviour at this time may take the form of self-injury. Cuts on the wrist are common, varying from scratches to deep lacerations made with a razor blade or broken glass. Sometimes the legs and genitals are sites of injury. The behaviour may be repeated frequently and be quite serious as in the case of Cecilia (see Chapter 3). She had extensive and lasting facial disfiguration as a result of repeated falls, and scars all over her body from self-injury. Oddly, however, she did not cut her wrists.

As in her case and so many of these girls' stories, one finds a broken home but more important a lack of warm and loving relationships. Most significantly there is an extreme distaste of menstruation, with problems of obtaining and disposing of sanitary towels, and self-injury occurs as each period begins. In some way cutting seems a means of relieving inner tension, anger and aggression. This may sometimes be turned on others, but it is mainly self-directed—oddly enough suicidal thoughts are not usually present. Experts feel that these girls are intent on self-injury apparently for its own sake. Many may not even come to the attention of psychiatrists.

In a community, for example a home for disturbed girls, or a psychiatric ward of a hospital devoted to adolescents, one self-injurer may cause a whole epidemic of similar behaviour. Sometimes there is mass fainting; such behaviour is often reported in the press as caused by a mystery virus, but in fact it is a curious form of what has loosely been called 'mass hysteria'.

When in the menstrual cycle?

It is tempting to relate a variety of conditions to the menstrual cycle, migraine and epilepsy being just two examples. Much attention has focused on the premenstrual stage, when women feel particularly tense—this is due to fluid retention related to hormonal changes. There can also be problems in the middle of the cycle when ovulation occurs.

Recently, there have been detailed studies of suicidal behaviour in French women either taking the contraceptive pill or not. Those on the pill showed no relationship between the menstrual cycle and drug overdose. But those *not* taking the pill had a higher incidence of attempted suicide.

The premenstrual time has been a target for much discussion, even used in court cases as mitigating circumstances to excuse widely differing antisocial behaviours ranging from shoplifting to murder. Of course, the majority of women do not appear to have any serious problems at this or other times during menstruation. But for those who do various forms of medical treatment are often helpful.

The stress of having a baby

Delivery is often a most stressful time, whether or not the mother wanted a child. The immediate reaction is of excitement, with husband or boyfriend, family and friends rallying around, but enthusiasm for the 'arrival' may quickly wane, and some mothers both young and old feel flat and unhappy for some time after they arrive home with the baby. These feelings are usually just a passing phase; worries about feeding, bathing or sudden death of the baby in the night evaporate with growing experience. The teenage mother with little support from the family, or on her own with an erratic boyfriend, finds coping less easy. However, with outside help from various sources she is often able to manage well.

There is a group of mothers whose feelings of sadness progress into severe depressive symptoms with serious disturbance in sleeping and eating habits. This is the condition of postnatal depression which, if not recognized, may have tragic results; the feeling of desperation and inability to cope may lead to murder of the baby, and possibly the mother's suicide.

Menopause

During this stage periods become erratic before they stop altogether. The menopause itself is particularly associated with actual bodily changes often exaggerated by worries about increasing age, loss of attractiveness to the opposite sex, compounded by weight gain. Tension and depression, sometimes with suicidal thoughts, are features. The use of hormone treatment is controversial, widely discussed particularly because of the potential risk of causing cancer when oestrogen preparations are used for long periods. But they do often eliminate both physical and mental symptoms of the menopause in women. Attempted suicide is less frequent than in younger women. But the figure for the number of women who actually kill themselves is rising with increasing age (as it is in men). The menopause is yet another life event that carries an underlying risk in suicide. The event that triggers the act is usually quite separate.

5

Teenage Suicides

An extremely worrying trend that has recently emerged is the increase in suicide in the young. This rising toll, particularly of teenage deaths, is worldwide and a cause for grave concern, not just because of age, but because it appears to stem from their obvious lack of self-esteem, and fulfilment. The problem has been particularly well documented in the United States, where not only the numbers but the bizarre pattern of multiple suicide pacts are very alarming. The considerable publicity these receive seems to cause widely imitative behaviour.

In the past, suicide in children and teenagers was regarded as comparatively rare. But today it is clear that even very young children do commit suicide—one only has to read newspaper accounts of children under ten from very disturbed backgrounds, often sexually abused, who had made unsuccessful efforts to seek help and finally killed themselves. One might argue that they were unaware of the meaning and finality of death and therefore form a different group from older suicides. But it must be accepted that they have deliberately brought about their end. They are obvious targets for prevention.

Teenage culture as we know it today began in the United States, and recently experts there have become aware that deaths between the ages of 15 and 25 represent an escalating proportion of suicidal fatalities. Since 1955 a threefold change has been found; the rate continues to accelerate, while suicide figures for all ages together have increased only marginally. (This crucial upturn must be put in perspective, because suicide in 70 and 80-year-olds still represents a greater actual number.)

Suicide pacts

Case history

The suicide pact is a particularly disturbing feature. Take this example: a 17-year-old and her sister with two similarly-aged companions drove to a petrol station at 3.0 am and bought petrol, asking the attendant if they could take the hose from the automobile vacuum cleaner; he wisely refused. They drove a short distance to an unoccupied garage, a known hangout for teenagers who drank excessively, and took drugs. With the car doors tight shut, but the windows open, they started the motor. A few hours later they were found dead. Unfortunately this incident, fully covered in the media, was not an isolated event, and sparked off a number of similar teenage pacts.

Warning signs

Teenagers, like others who sadly kill themselves, have shown warning signs. How can these be spotted? A deteriorating work record at school is often an early sign, perhaps leading to dropping out of high school. This sign is often coupled with evidence of depression, loss of interest in clothes, hair, and boyfriends, usually so important to the teenager. There may have been previous suicidal attempts of varying severity, girls often slashing their wrists or taking a few tablets. Recently drug and alcohol abuse tend to be coupled with these other signs, but even the experts state categorically that recognition of real problems leading to suicide can be much more difficult than in mature adults.

Prevention training

In the United States, because of worry over the shocking cases such as the example above, counselling networks were begun, suicide prevention training was given to teachers and students, telephone hotlines were opened and parent awareness programmes begun, to help spot potential victims. Here too we must now change our attitudes. It has been shown that understanding and help, particularly in young women, can prevent disaster. This is discussed further in Chapter 8.

6

The Underlying Causes

In this chapter we shall look at some of the underlying causes of the feelings of hopelessness and desperation that lead to suicide.

The angry suicide

In his book *Living with Grief* Tony Lake suggests that anger is one of the commonest emotions in suicide. Strong, violent and destructive feelings are very basic; as a child one is aware of frustration when a favourite toy stops working, and is then smashed against the floor or perhaps against the child itself. The hurt causes pain and leads to crying, shouting, screaming, violent emotions encompassed in anger. Jill (see Chapter 1) was angry with her boyfriend when he criticized her, and Stewart (see Chapter 1) was frustrated by his physical illness and angry with his wife for dying. An all-pervasive anger and aggression against those left behind is found in almost every suicide: 'I will show them what I really meant.' 'How will they feel about me when I'm gone?'

Escape from fear and pain

However, when the aggressive feelings are exhausted, it is fear of life that is dominant. Stewart (see Chapter 1) was not only angry, but was afraid of what he had to face: 'How can I get through the winter with no one to help, nobody caring; if I'm snowed in, I cannot drive the car.' The pain and hopelessness is also shown in the much younger man, Edward (see Chapter 1), who after a highly successful business career was made redundant. This not only caused marked loss of self-esteem, but also financial problems for a family accustomed to a high income. Recurrence of a previous depressive illness was a pointer to the inevitability of suicide.

Those who wish to escape from pain and fear often choose a peaceful method of death—tablets, drowning or gassing—in order to leave their bodies whole. The sentiments may sometimes be coupled with anger: 'You did not do enough for me when I was here'. For those left this makes the coping difficult, a point to which we will return in Chapter 10.

Underlying causes

Now we must concentrate on two other factors in suicide—underlying reasons, and immediate precipitants.

Stewart was bereaved and the pain created by this coupled with the burden of various physical problems—arthritic hip, hernia, tinnitus, heart and urinary problems—all contributed. What, in fact was the trigger here? The failure of the urinary operation was the most likely.

Of all the principal causes mental illness, usually depression, is the one that emerges most often, as well as personality problems which have never been resolved. These include drug addiction, alcohol, and compulsive gambling; taken together they account for over half the instances. Marital, sexual and family difficulties, particularly coping with children, loom large as underlying factors.

26

The *actual* trigger to a suicidal episode is often less clear. To the outsider a tiff with a boyfriend, the arrival of a small gas bill, a phone call from the school about a child's non-attendance, the failure of a relative to offer an invitation at Christmas, all pale into insignificance compared with the enormity of self-destruction. Yet if on close examination afterwards there seems nothing else we must conclude that in some people these are sufficient causes.

Expert views

Because suicide is such a difficult topic, experts from a variety of backgrounds have struggled in an attempt to make sense of what seems nonsense.

Durkheim

At the end of the last century the celebrated sociologist Durkheim attempted to find a pattern. He talked of egotistical suicide, where a person had lost hold and concern for life in the world around and sought an end to it all—the physically and mentally ill and bereaved, for instance. He also saw another pattern—those who had lost their religious, professional and marital standards, for various reasons. This had to be seen against the background of the very rigid Victorian era. There was in his view yet another kind who truly see their suicides as a sacrifice for others. Everyone now seems to regard such a pattern as rare, but we shall return to this below.

Baechler

In this century, Baechler, also a sociologist, put forward a whole range of other ideas which have widened our understanding—escapism, flight from illness—and he regarded grief, real or imagined, as important. Faults and failings, aggressive behaviour, violence and even blackmail also form part of the complex pattern. Of course, all these ideas are mixed up with feelings and actions in non-suicides, but become of vital importance in the contemplation of suicide.

Sacrifice and suicide

The idea of 'letting go' is present in many suicides—for instance, Stewart's suicide note: 'You will be better off when I'm dead'. Death is a means of escape, but at the same time in some way helps those who are left ('You will be better off when I'm gone'). In religious terms this can be described as 'sacrifice', such as like the marytrs make in dying for their beliefs. Jan Palach, the Czech student who set fire to himself in 1968, can be regarded as a sort of secular martyr. The most striking fictional example is Sidney Carton in Charles Dickens's *Tale of Two Cities*, who went to the guillotine so that another might live saying, 'This is a far, far better thing that I do now than I have ever done; it is a far, far better rest I go to now than I have ever known.'

Famous sacrifices abound: Sir Philip Sidney giving his water bottle to a dying soldier on the battlefield saying, 'Thy need is yet greater than mine'; Captain Oates's famous last words on Scott's doomed South Polar expedition: 'I am going out now, and I may be some time'—on frostbitten feet he limped to certain death in a blizzard, believing that his death would help the Polar party to reach safety.

These actions clearly raise the whole question as to whether 'normal' people ever commit suicide. It is a subject of great controversy even amongst experts and can never be totally resolved.

Gambling with death

A view held by some can be simply expressed as: 'Unless you gamble with death you have not really lived'. The idea that life is a gamble and must be played for high stakes is a recurring theme, found in various fields, from pop music to high finance. American teenagers play games on motorways; children in the East End of London charge fearlessly across the busy Whitechapel Road where I work. It also exists in a highly dangerous form—Russian roulette.

Case history: Max

Max, in his 20s, had never really known his father due to the latter's frequent absences from home on account of his maritime work, and then an early divorce. He fantasized his father as the Captain of an oceangoing liner. His mother, charming, vivacious, life-and-soul-of-the-party, loved everyone and wanted to *be* loved by everyone. She smothered her son to the extent that he ran away becoming a policeman in Brunei and marrying one of the local beauties. He, too, loved and had to be loved. Max played for high stakes in work, and with women, drink and money. This led quickly to corruption, so common then in the Far East. One day he was found dead. His police revolver contained live bullets, but also two duds. Max had spoken briefly of his desperation to a lover, but it was not until his death when debts were revealed that one could appreciate the depths to which he had sunk.

Slow self-destruction

Also important in suicide are the slow, self-destructive processes, amounting almost to suicide. These are often quite obvious to the onlooker—wife, relative, or close friend—and yet the individual is totally unaware of them. If there *is* any sudden flash of awareness this is at once pushed to the back of the mind, totally out of conscious thought. Addiction to alcohol and drugs are examples which if continued to excess inevitably end in death. This could be regarded as amounting almost as clearly to suicide, as actually taking a drug overdose. Watching the decline is painful, but trying to change the ingrained pattern is normally extremely difficult.

We have also seen examples in our own lives as well as through the media's eyes. Drug addiction, for example, is paraded before us daily in the newspapers or on television often in an almost glamorous way. Pop stars, film stars rise and fall. In all cases it is close friends and family who have the power to help. So in our own everyday life we must look around and note those who are on this path of self-destruction, unrecognized by themselves. Sometimes, often with difficulty, we can help, for there are many ways of self-destruction.

Anorexia nervosa

In anorexia nervosa—the slimmer's disease—a young woman, apparently considering herself overweight (which is not usually the case), goes on a strict diet. She loses weight and then a pattern of binging and dieting alternates (also present in bulimia nervosa). Even when she eats a meal with friends or family, almost as she finishes she induces vomiting to rid herself of the food. Soon, of course, she weighs perhaps 30 kg (5 or 6 stone), medically a very dangerous condition.

Case history: Wendy

Wendy was a top model when she became anorexic. In her case the death of a 'love child' started an obsession with food and figure coupled with a compulsive urge to destroy herself. She blamed herself for the loss of the baby and hated her body. She took an overdose of tablets and alcohol, but was discovered in her hotel room and lived. Then began the long and difficult course of treatment, so often the case. Wendy survived, but many do not, dying of the effects of starvation or infection which take hold due to the body's poor resistance.

Other causes

The acquired immune deficiency syndrome (AIDS) is becoming an increasing reason for committing suicide. Curiously, suicidal feelings are more common when a person initially discovers that he is HIV-positive, rather than later when death is inevitable.

The persistence of promiscuous sexual activity is fraught with disaster and the odds of contracting AIDS, though they may not be as high as Russian roulette, are increasing daily.

In terms of numbers, alcohol is the most potent addictive drug, and it is found in all levels of society. The Royal College of Physicians calls it 'our favourite addictive drug'. It plays an important part not just in an ongoing destructive pattern but also very often in the final act of suicide. The long-term action of alcohol causes both physical and intellectual decline.

7

The Methods of Suicide

We are of course interested in how the individual may be prevented from committing suicide, so in this chapter we shall consider the various ways in which death may be brought about.

At first glance the methods of suicide available appear to be numerous. In practice, the choice is limited because much suicidal behaviour is impulsive, and only carefully planned for the minority. Accessibility varies with many factors, for example living in the country or having a specific occupation. Domestic gas was once lethal, but this is no longer the case. Deadly carbon monoxide fumes from cars have only represented a risk in this century. Nowadays in many countries, a notable exception being the United States, there is very strict firearm control. However, availability is clearly only one aspect; jumping from high places or into the path of fastmoving trains or lorries is readily within the reach of most and would be expected to be the most frequent method. But though these means are important they do not figure very highly; obviously they are too violent.

Violent versus non-violent means

As we saw earlier, some who commit suicide choose a way so their body may be preserved intact, whereas in others this is not the case. For this reason it is usual to think of two distinct means: violent and non-violent.

A combination of methods used together are not

uncommon, for example an overdose of medication with alcohol and subsequent drowning.

The detached observer familiar with detective stories may imagine that a swift sure method would be easy to achieve. However, as with murder, this is not so. So often there are loopholes, sometimes intentional, which are obvious to the family, relations and friends, so fortunately many attempts are stopped in their tracks.

In Stewart's case (see Chapter 1) one can subsequently piece together in some detail all the events that led to his end. A neighbour told the family that he was clearly disturbed. He spent some weeks of effort in obtaining the means and planning his method. He was rejected at a gunsmiths where he had attempted to buy a weapon, but later he changed his tack and returned to the local hardware shop twice to obtain the appropriate length of rope. On two separate occasions, once in the attic and once in the garage, he was discovered searching for what turned out to be a convenient jumping point for his death by hanging. He was determined to die.

Violent means of suicide such as hanging, shooting, knives and other instruments are more characteristic of men than women, while drowning and jumping from a high place are the opposite. The use of such methods has decreased with a corresponding increase in the use of medicines, a pattern common to most European countries, Australia and the United States.

Drug overdose

In most developed countries the commonest method used in suicide and attempted suicide is poisoning. Medication prescribed by doctors, such as hypnotics and tranquillizers, or 'over-the-counter' products such as aspirin and para-cetamol are swallowed. Though this method represents only a small proportion of all suicides it is clearly a matter in which controls are possible, and these have recently been introduced in the United Kingdom. These drug deaths, taken together with other poisonings, domestic, industrial and from car exhaust fumes, form the most common cause of deaths both for men and women. The use of these has increased over the years since 1955 by as much as three times.

Knives and domestic strife

Many suicide attempts (and homicides too) occur in a domestic setting. It is obvious that dangerous objects around the house, and in the kitchen particularly, figure largely. A knife grabbed in anger in the heat of an argument is a very nasty weapon. It can cause both a mortal injury to another person, or self-injury. The potential risk for the housewife almost every minute of every day is demonstrated by the frequency with which kitchen knives figure in obsessional ruminative conditions. Such a disorder is a form of severe neurosis in which there is a constant intense fear that a knife may be used to harm or even kill someone else in the household. This fear is so enveloping that the person concerned is unable to carry on a normal life.

Case history: Lisa

Lisa was a minister's wife, a missionary abroad, when after the birth of her first child, a girl, she was struck by a severe incapacitating knife phobia. She was the apple of her father's eye, an adoration which grew with age and her attractiveness. In Lisa's thoughts the knife was directed at both her child and her husband. Returning home to England and having another child, combined with skilled professional help, prevented what could have been both murder and suicide combined.

8

The Warning Signs

Warnings of intention

Whatever the method of suicide used, warnings, often repeated, are given before the final act, quite contrary to general belief. For example, more than three-quarters of a group studied in the United States had indicated their intentions to someone close, and often more than once. Other psychiatrists' figures are almost as high. The majority of the deceased received medical or psychiatric treatment within a year of their death. This is another indication of the mixed motives of even the most determined individuals.

We must therefore always take warnings seriously, even when they are given so frequently by, for example, depressed patients that it is difficult to know how to act. Indeed almost everyone at one or other time in their life may have had suicidal feelings, usually extremely vague, in contrast to the often fairly precise statements made by those who subsequently commit suicide. The number of times, the intensity and the certainty of the statement are revealing and they provide a platform for positive action.

It is important to note if there are any other changes suggesting bodily or mental disturbance taking the form of physical complaints such as headaches, stomach pain, and poor appetite; coupled with poor concentration, lack of interest in work, family and hobbies, and poor sleep these are all signs. More details are given later in this chapter.

Recognition

Spotting the person in need, family or friend, is the first means we have of recognizing a potential suicide or attempted suicide. When several disastrous life events occur within a short space of time—bereavement, illness and redundancy, for example—then beware. The signs are often quite clear but we may not take heed.

Ordinary signs like the constant pale face, the tense look, poor sleep, loss of appetite, untidy appearance are features. But this can be quite difficult to recognize because the change is often rather gradual. The same suit or tie worn every day in a snappy, careful dresser, a subtle change from bright to darker colours, may be clues. I always look at the colour of patients' clothes when he or she enters the clinic if I know that there is a tendency to depression. Walking slowly, and a quiet, barely audible voice may be just the first signs of a vast number of ways of communicating with each other without words. Facial make-up, closeness or not of shave, uncut and dirty finger nails, straggly hair, scruffy or dirty shoes, are all telltale signs of trouble brewing.

Signs of depression

Domestically, there are such features as loss of interest in usually pleasurable pursuits, changes in concentration and a constant concern that everything is not up to standard. Restlessness and irritability are part of some people's nature, but exaggeration of these characteristics indicates depression.

Inner depressive thoughts reveal themselves as concentration on morbid subjects, such as sad or unpleasant stories in the newspapers, or on television, or talk of death or anniversaries of death. Hopelessness and pessimism about the future are particularly marked in those with a real wish to die. They may talk vaguely about people and objects acting against them; or say that they are unworthy and have been evil in the past. The ideas are quite out of proportion and this is an important clue; mention of suicide itself and how it might be done is also a vital telltale sign. Don't forget that three-quarters of those people who kill themselves will have given hints of this, often many times in the days before the event.

Constant physical illness, odd persistent complaints, unaffected by the usual painkillers or medicine from the doctors, are other features. Again the majority of people committing suicide have sought medical help, and many have been in hospital for investigation and treatment prior to their suicide. Knowledge of earlier depressive episodes is also of particular importance.

Sometimes there are reasons why we do not want to recognize the warning signs. Maybe our concern in the past was misplaced. But if we suspect something is wrong, it is vital to pursue the feeling. If we say, for example: 'You look a bit down today', or 'things not too good?' this may encourage them to reveal the dismal nature of their inner thoughts and possible concerns about suicide.

Seeking help

After recognizing that there is a problem, help must be sought for the individual, initially from the family doctor. Friends and colleagues who are concerned have a demanding task; they have to persuade the person that they need help, convince them that they have changed in the ways described above and are obviously depressed. If they still will not go to a doctor or hospital emergency department on their own, a friend or colleague should take them, or consider contacting an organization such as the Samaritans.

Recognizing the means available

Whatever the social setting at this point, there must be careful consideration of what is available as a means of bringing about a possible suicide. The most obvious is supplies of medicines either prescribed or bought over the counter. The person should obviously be watched carefully and, depending on the severity of the situation must not be allowed to go out alone to perhaps buy supplies of tablets, or jump off a high building, or dash out into the path of moving traffic.

Keep them talking

A person thinking of suicide will have many ideas bottled up inside—some strange and even bizarre. The very mention of the word 'suicide' if the subject has not been broached by someone else may be difficult. The first step therefore is to open up this subject and then let the other person do the talking. This is crucial to the work of the Samaritans (see Chapter 11).

At first, when dealing with someone you think may be suicidal discussion of deep philosophical subjects—such as the purpose of the universe, or the ethical aspects of euthanasia—may seem to be important. But this is often a blind alley. Bear in mind that the person who insists that they want to die, and have a right to die which nobody can take away, is usually seriously depressed. There may be no tears, no talk of sadness, no odd notions of persecution, but depression nevertheless is lurking there underneath. Your aim is to make the person feel that, in spite of everything, they have something to live for.

Talking about religion can be a double-edged weapon. If the person is a believer in God, a life hereafter may be something wished for, perhaps so they can be happy and join loved ones. We should emphasize, however, that in most religions, even if they foster the view of the importance of existence hereafter or even the chance to return to another life on earth, the supreme purpose is being *here*. This is an important topic to pursue. If the situation seems desperate, offer the help needed at once; tomorrow may be too late.

The doctor's role in prevention

If one puts oneself in the position of a person intent on suicide, and tries to imagine what there is at hand to perform the act, it becomes obvious that the possibilities are limitless. After the event many people feel that they should have foreseen these possibilities and taken action such as perhaps mounting a 24-hour guard. Commonsense shows that this is usually impossible. However, it does not mean that we should not take simple precautions—for example, tablets prescribed should be hidden and given out in the prescribed dose a few at a time.

Doctors aware of problems write a prescription for small amounts of antidepressants or only allow it to be picked up every few days from the chemist. In any case anti-depressants are themselves much less dangerous than sedatives such as barbiturates. Large bottles of aspirin or other painkillers should not be in the house; 50 or 100 tablets of this kind if taken are damaging if not fatal. Someone in a suicidal frame of mind can easily obtain such supplies over the chemist's counter, so shopping trips should be supervised, but what about kitchen knives? These are dangerous but it is almost impossible for them to be kept out of sight all the time.

Consider, too, what dangers lie outside the home—high buildings, bridges, fastmoving traffic, are readily available if the person is really determined, but even here there are controls. Bus drivers and underground train drivers are vigilant when passengers are very near the kerb or edge of the platform. Police are on the watch for those who climb up high bridges or buildings, and it is quite clear that even those who have taken themselves to dangerous places do not necessarily act at once. We read in the papers of many would-be suicides who are 'talked down', so even here a period of time exists in which action can be taken.

Bringing risks into the open

Our difficulties revolve around not so much what is available, but assessing the risk. How can we know the danger signs and recognize the utter despair? At this point, it is important if you feel there is a serious risk simply to bring it out in the open.

'You don't look well today.' 'Nerves bad?' 'How bad, very bad?' 'Are you very depressed?' 'Have you thought of ending it all, doing away with yourself?'

These kinds of remarks can bring out the real feelings and the immediate action to be taken. It may produce a flood of tears and relief that someone really understands. At this point do *not* say, 'Promise me you won't do anything silly.' A very depressed, suicidal person cannot

42

promise this any more than a heroin addict can promise that they will not have another fix. You should say: 'I will come and see you later today or give you a ring.' If the situation seems less serious say: 'Give me a ring anytime to talk things over.'

9

Mercy Killing

The subject of mercy killing, or euthanasia, has for some time occupied many doctors who justly have the right to be concerned because of their exceptionally wide experience of suicidal behaviour. Stated bluntly, one could ask of the experts: are there any circumstances in which a person who expressed with full conviction a desire to commit suicide is ever sane? Further, if so, should a doctor offer help?

There are real problems here—the doctor's Hippocratic Oath for a start. It is in order for the doctor not to strive unduly to keep a patient alive, but actually to assist in bringing about death is another matter. In such an action the doctor perhaps puts himself on a par with God. He is deciding that this particular life has no longer any value, its quality is so impaired that absence is better than even tainted continuation. Many doctors say simply, 'No'. In their view, to connive with suicide is to fail the patient by confirming despair, denying hope and abandoning further treatment.

In my view in many circumstances this is right. For the patient to reach this level of desperation it is obvious that medical and non-medical help has failed.

Background to euthanasia

In 1961 the 'Suicide Act' was passed and attempted suicide was no longer a crime. With the change in attitude to suicide, there was also a change in attitude to mercy killing—euthanasia—a gentle and easy death brought about particularly in the case of incurable and painful diseases. For such an idea to gain root there must be safeguards, and it must be the clear desire of the individual involved. This motion was put forward as long ago as 1935 when the Voluntary Euthanasia Society was founded. It has continued to be supported by many famous proponents, not only the eminent in every walk of life but also many doctors and psychiatrists. It is permitted in Holland, though each case has to be reported to a coroner to be assessed.

The BMA working party report

A working party of The British Medical Association examined all aspects of the subject and reported their findings in mid 1988. In summary, their report, while recognizing that euthanasia may well, in practice, happen, recommends it should remain illegal in Britain.

The working party had a wide brief including a review of the law in this country relating to both suicide and homicide. It examined what is done in other countries, for example the United States, where similar studies are in progress, and having examined the trends in public opinion in the United Kingdom set out its views as to what should be done.

There is a remarkable public interest in this subject. A survey carried out in 1985 found that 72 per cent agreed that adults should receive medical help towards death if they suffered from an incurable physical disease which was intolerable to them—but only if the person had already given his wish for help *in writing*.

On the whole medical opinion was more guarded; 35 per cent of family doctors said they would consider supporting the idea of voluntary euthanasia if the law were changed, and a further 10 per cent of these general practitioners indicated that they may consider such a possibility. Just over a half said they would not. As the Voluntary Euthanasia Society points out, this means that approximately 13,500 view voluntary euthanasia positively. There has been particular support for euthanasia in patients dying of AIDS. Increasing numbers of people are suffering from AIDS, although there are hopes of a cure in the future. Medical help can only offer some amelioration, bearing in mind that the terminal stages of this disease are extremely depressing and unpleasant.

Patients with terminal cancer

Advanced cancer is the example generally put forward in defence of the idea of euthanasia or at least allowing and helping the patient to die. There are provisos: there must be no serious emotional distress amounting to psychiatric illness, which in any case is usually amenable to drug treatment; the reasons for asking to die must be valid not only to the sick patient and his or her relatives, but also to the majority of the community at large for them to accept this view as reasonable.

If we study cancer victims who seem appropriate candidates for euthanasia, we find that the suicide rate is *lower* rather than higher as might have been expected, so the matter is not so straightforward.

Another point to bear in mind is the inherent risk that exists if the idea of mercy killing is widely adopted. The cancer victim might even feel obliged to commit suicide to free his or her relatives from an intolerable burden.

Kinds of mercy killing

Let us now turn to the different kinds of mercy killing. Many of its supporters would take the view that it is better to bring the whole matter clearly into the open with the sufferers and allow a gentle and easy death with the help of caring relatives and professionals.

Voluntary euthanasia

If the individual indicates his or her desire to die and there is no compulsion, this is called 'voluntary euthanasia'. A crucial point is whether or not the person has control of his mental faculties at the time. Such a situation has been taken care of by use of 'the living will'. For someone with an incurable condition, such a document is signed by the person ahead of time; it can be used when the end of the road is reached in medical treatment.

This is only one aspect; the other concerns whether treatment should be withdrawn or some positive step taken to hasten death. The doctor does not strive unnecessarily to prolong life and uses powerful drugs to control severe pain. These may in themselves hasten death, but this is not why they are used. On the other hand, he could, in the view of those who favour euthanasia, take a direct action to end life.

Passive euthanasia

In passive euthanasia the doctor, after discussion, discontinues antibiotics which could, for example, cure a lung infection in someone suffering from an incurable disease. Or in the case of a patient who has suffered severe brain injury, for example following a road traffic accident, the doctor turns off the ventilator which is maintaining the patient's breathing.

Active euthanasia

When the question of active means to end life is raised, so-called 'active euthanasia', the main concerns, doubts, fears and dilemmas are raised.

The experience in Holland

In Holland the whole subject of active euthanasia has been tackled 'head on'. Euthanasia has a legally accepted status, and in recent years 5000 or 6000 people have had an easy, gentle death. Dr Peter Admiraal is one of active euthanasia's most active proponents. His views arise from his wide experience with the terminally ill in the hospice situation, where individual care is carefully tailored to the patient's needs with the use of appropriate painkilling drugs and other therapy. It was from this background that his practice of euthanasia arose. He points out that whereas the pain itself is often treatable the complete loss of dignity and the suffering that comes with conditions other than those producing pain are *not* acceptable, and are the main reason for people wanting to die peacefully. He gives examples: 'growths that choke, produce constant thirst and unbearable itching'. Of course he accepts that passive means of euthanasia are often appropriate, turning off the respirator, discontinuing tube feeding or kidney dialysis, but with his extensive knowledge and experience he has developed the means of administering drugs which bring a speedy end.

On the legal side, the official attitude in Holland has been to use a set of detailed guidelines brought out in 1981.

Here are just some examples of the points included: the physical or mental suffering must be lasting and unbearable to the patient; the patient must be in full possession of the facts and his decision must be voluntary; the time and manner of death must not cause misery to others; the next of kin should be informed in advance of the decision; the patient's affairs be in reasonable order; and so on.

Equally important is the fact that the decision to give 'aid-in-dying' must not be taken by a single person, and another doctor not involved directly in the case must be consulted. Obviously the drugs must be presented by a doctor and their administration surrounded with the utmost care. Perhaps the most radical aspect is that the patient need not necessarily be *terminally* ill. Those with severe incapacitating diseases such as complete paralysis of the lower half of the body (paraplegia) may be eligible for euthanasia.

The experience in the United States

Many state laws allow 'competent' patients the right to refuse medical care. The so-called 'living will' (see page 47) allows patients to provide written instructions about what types of medical intervention they wish or do not wish to receive if they become incompetent. This means that patients can refuse, or doctors withhold, the use of kidney dialysis or other forms of treatment to maintain life including tube and intravenous feeding. Perhaps more controversial, but again supported by laws of various states, if the patient is incompetent then parents, for example, may give consent for such action.

What now in the United Kingdom?

In the United Kingdom the attitude is one of 'hastening

slowly' and the time is not quite at hand for active euthanasia. Having read much and thought deeply on the subject before writing this chapter, I feel that we must seriously consider active euthanasia. But for the present I suggest it is important to clarify the issues surrounding passive euthanasia, improving the care of the terminally sick before considering the more active approach. Probably this will be considered first for those who are terminally ill, and might be acceptable in those with degenerative disorders of the brain, such as Alzheimer's disease; but it will be a considerable time before those with, for example, paraplegia, will be actively given drugs to bring about a speedy death, if they request it. The 'living will' (page 47), now accepted in many countries, is one important issue.

These matters have, sadly, not been resolved by the 1988 report of the BMA working party. Euthanasia remains a subject of controversy and debate in this country.

10

The Aftermath

Whatever the cause of a death in someone close to us the effect is overwhelming, and extremely difficult to explain. 'Shock' is the word that comes to mind, but it is found so often in newspaper headlines that its impact has been lost. The aftermath of death by suicide and the emotions that result are particularly difficult to resolve. I shall attempt to indicate the problems using my own experience as well as that of friends, patients, and the writings of others. Dr Lake's book, *Living with Grief*, is particularly recommended.

The first blow

The telephone rang. It was 8.30 pm. An unfamiliar voice (a policeman) told me, without emotion, that my father, Stewart, had hanged himself in his garage.

I remember the moment well, I was transfixed, immobile, unable to speak. The policeman had repeatedly to jolt me before I could reply. Tears flowed down my cheeks as I closed the conversation: 'No, I do not want to hear the suicide note read tonight. Tomorrow morning I will ring you. Goodnight.'

The first minutes, hours and days are quite different from what follows later. Shock and sadness tinged with disbelief are the main themes at first. Yet, as in my case and in many others, there was already a note of *knowing* what the telephone conversation would bring, an element of inevitability that produced a seed of guilt which was to grow. If the event seemed inevitable, why was nothing done to prevent it? Of course this is only part of the problem, as there is much more to do than coping emotionally.

Practical matters

In the early days practical things must be done. In spite of the extreme sadness and strong disbelief one is carried along by events. I recall clearly saying, if not out loud, but to myself over and over again, 'He was alive 24 hours ago'. I was spared the identification of his body which many have to face; this can be a most unpleasant task. Relatives and friends rally round; some may feel revulsion about the manner of death, but the closest and dearest see the horror and help.

After the post mortem, a necessity in suicide cases, acceptance by the coroner of the cause of death means that the death certificate is signed and funeral arrangements can be made. Here again, though there is a welling up of emotion, details are usually carried through swiftly. Undertakers, with their experience and calm assurance, are extremely helpful and reassuring.

A word about the outward expression of grief: it is a good thing to cry, indeed not only quite acceptable but also understood and even expected. The idea that women weep and men keep a stiff upper lip belongs to the past. We see on the television almost every day after harrowing political and natural events leading to death how people react in a way that, say, thirty years ago would have been unthinkable.

When arranging the funeral there may be conflict within the family about church or synagogue versus a civil ceremony. Then there may be questions about memorial services, when and where they should be held, how they should be conducted, and what should be said, but by that stage much will have happened and feelings will have changed considerably.

Friends and relatives, whether verbally or in letters, are at pains to avoid the comments that must be in their minds. What they really want to say is: 'Why did you allow it to happen?', 'How terrible of him to do this.' These feelings are within ourselves as well but become much stronger later. At this stage the person grieving is buoyed up by necessary events—family gatherings, meetings of old friends and acquaintances. An almost party spirit prevails, and yet inevitably the single feeling of sadness is more mixed and complicated than when the death is from natural causes.

Another practical problem is what is to become of the dead person's belongings. This is hard to face up to. It is important, however, to keep some—a few mementoes—don't get rid of them all. Wiping the slate clean in this way is a sign of non-acceptance rather than coping.

Suicide notes

Feelings of bewilderment and helplessness are uppermost especially when there is a suicide note. Its presence is important, because at the legal level, this indicates that the coroner will almost certainly record a verdict of death by suicide. But it is the response created in the receiver rather than the coroner's verdict which is important.

At this stage perhaps some may be comforted by the findings of the experts who have studied the contents of suicide notes. First, they are found after about a quarter of deaths; older people rather than younger tend to commit their thoughts to paper, in keeping with their greater understanding of the complexity of life and the seriousness of their intentions. However, the contents are invariably written under extreme emotional stress, an important point for those who receive them. They are the views of the moment, tinged with all the emotional colours that might be expected, and *must not be seen as the whole truth*.

They are usually bold expressions of love and hate, often mixed, also aggression and revenge coupled with the desire for love, affection and forgiveness. Perhaps curiously, reference to the motive of suicide is not universal. The writers concentrate on what is going to happen *after* their death. The future looms large—why should this be? It is perhaps not really unexpected, for in those who survive a suicide attempt there is a relief of tension and depression and in some almost a feeling of elation.

Surprisingly, the contents of the note may not seem to accept the inevitability of the action. The writer is continuing to play a role in the actual world. He or she may blame society at large, but may also seek forgiveness for his/her actions from those who are close. In my father's case he suggested that things would be better for us after he had gone: 'You may not see it like that now, but you will.' This type of comment is often found. He, like so many, had a preoccupation with the living world.

The first few days

After hearing of my father's suicide I found that work, so far as it was possible within the restraints of coping with the inevitable physical turmoil, was my main stabilizing factor. True, family, friends and colleagues were utterly supportive, yet I continued to feel horrified by the event. As time passed the emotions became more mixed, muddled and contradictory. He was dead, no one denied that, but why *now*? He had been due to come and stay with us only a few days after the event. I felt a complex mixture of resentment and self-pity. It was only later that the negative feelings subsided. Then self-pity gave way to true appreciation of the significance of his action. Finally, but very much later, acceptance of what had happened began to emerge. When this point is reached, there is a feeling almost of thanksgiving. The loved one, in spite of everything, is at peace.

The beginning of acceptance

Thoughts very soon after the news of death by suicide almost always contain the 'if only' aspect—I should have telephoned, written or invited him or her round. At the same time the 'I knew what the message was going to be about' springs up (as in my case)—there had been a constant worry since you last said 'goodbye' that it would be the final time.

Then comes the realization that you will never see the person again. Was it really true? Could there be a mistake? The pattern of bereavement dealing with the problems and emotions that are aroused is similar whether the death is by suicide or from natural causes. So for everyone the first important part of acceptance is that the death has really happened. The relationship you have had with the one now dead was in some senses a failure. Yet it is not over. Life takes on a new form, but anger too is a natural outcome, not to be ignored or denied. The fact that the person committed suicide shows up your helplessness, making you both guilty and angry.

Guilt

A father said after the death of his son: 'I was full of remorse, full of the things I felt I should have done. I felt he had been crying out for help and I had not given enough—it was a kind of torture in my mind thinking about it.'

Is this self-punishment and guilt really necessary and how does it arise? Guilt is something learnt, present since early childhood, part of the way parents control us. If you have grasped this there is no longer a need for self-punishment. Guilt is inbuilt, starting in childhood and continuing into adult life. As we mature it has much wider implications so, for example, the death of one's own son can cause feelings of extreme guilt. In close relationships, where a sense of responsibility and partnership have been developed, a similar guilt is generated. What was the situation of the death? Would a phone call, a letter, really have made all that difference? How did it actually happen? Was it planned so that anyone could intervene?

Getting rid of the guilt means seeing that though the relationship appears now to have ended, it can and should take a new turn. The past should be viewed in a new light—the happy moments, the funny, or hectic times, everything that makes up a total relationship.

Talking out the guilt

It can be an embarrassment to talk about death and bereavement. But we should never shy away from discussing it, and being positive to others in a similar situation. In this way death can be a learning experience for us, a way of 'growing up' to the realization and consequences of living. Husbands or wives may not at first talk frankly to each other about a death or suicide, but this block must be overcome. Just as we have learnt our first faltering steps as a child trying to walk, so we must begin to learn acceptance. Only this way can we overcome guilt.

A positive outlook

Positive action, of course, only comes little by little, particularly at a time when everyone else around may be feeling depressed. Don't resort to drugs or drink. Their use can get out of hand, as solace at a time of real crisis, and eventually one may not be able to cope at all without them. Gain strength—fatigue and poor sleeping may be profound with bereavement. Take up new pursuits.

Realizing, too, that death has ended your duties to someone close, suicide being the sign that the relationship was at crisis point, can now give you freedom. Grief is the best way of restoring the true bonds of that memorable association. Melting of negative feelings leads to real gain. Something can always be learnt even from an overwhelming catastrophe.

Guidelines for coping

Grief is painful but coping is essential for one's own health, mental and physical, for personal growth and understanding of life in general. Here are some of the guidelines to use as pointers and reminders in the stages one has to go through. Acceptance is the first step. Asking questions 'why' and 'why not' do not help. Realization that one of our main concerns is confronting our own mortality and vulnerability, we must face these head on. Turn away from anger, guilt, fear and sadness to trust and hope. I must, of course, add that all this is easier said than done.

The next stage is to seek help, maybe of a professional kind. Some sources are listed in Chapter 11.

Family and friends will help pick up the pieces. Couple this with forgiveness and accepting the defects in yourself and the dead person. Remember with love what the relationship was like.

With as much strength as you can muster, turn next to making positive decisions; do what is necessary, step by step. Each new move and achievement will make the next bigger jump easier. Pay the bills, sort out the belongings. With these and other small decisions, confidence in yourself and your capabilities will grow.

Attempt to give life a fresh look, try to laugh, escape from the stale routine, take a new challenge, meet new people. Value the opportunities that family and friends may offer to drag you from your rut. However, do not at this stage make *big* decisions. Take small ones little by little, go away for a day or a weekend—but not a world cruise!

Finally, remember that grief and mourning have a *natural* course, but it takes time. As one counsellor put it: 'A journey through grief, taken in a series of steps, becomes a journey of discovery of yourself. . . . Make yourself better not bitter.'

11

Sources of Help

If you are seriously contemplating suicide you need help. It is a big problem but there is no shirking the reality. By the time you have come to this stage, when the help that family and friends can give is exhausted, you must get expert assistance. DON'T DELAY. Though it is tempting to believe that the feelings you have will go away, they may not, and in fact may get worse.

If you are a relation or friend of a seriously depressed person who is a suicidal risk, seek help—but from whom? The options are given below.

The family doctor

Maybe you have tried the family doctor, but have you given him a *real* idea of the desperation you feel? He is not a mind reader and can only respond to your needs if he is truly aware of them. Remember that you can talk to him even if you do not like him or feel that he has not helped in the past. He has access to various sources of help which you may not have thought of, or considered possible or useful. He has the skill to help with all the basic problems, be they deep down, family or sexual, excessive drinking, drug-taking, or most likely a serious underlying depressive illness that makes the coping seem impossible.

Drug therapy

The family doctor may decide to prescribe antidepressants. There are many kinds, and may be effective in alleviating even the worst depressive symptoms, though they may take a week to ten days to reach their peak effect. The tablets are often taken last thing at night so any sedative action aids sleep and has gone by the morning, but the mood-elevating effect is then at its maximum, just when things often seem at their blackest. Antidepressant tablets are not addictive and are quite different from the benzodiazepines that have recently received a bad press. Antidepressants are very effective when taken *for a limited period*, particularly if tension and agitation are special problems, as they can be in severe depression.

Counselling

Your family doctor may also have access to social workers and counsellors who can help, and will arrange for an appointment. Or the doctor may decide that referral to a psychiatrist is appropriate, and such a course of action should be accepted.

The psychiatrist

People often dread the word 'psychiatrist'. It seems to be linked with the most bizarre forms of madness, or distorted views. But he is the most likely person to be able to assist a potential suicide.

The psychiatrist has vast experience of the range of depressive symptoms and the form they take. He/she can assess the problems more accurately than the family doctor. He can choose from the wide range of anti-depressants the most appropriate because of its particular action on, for example, sleeplessness or agitation.

He has access to a wide range of helpers who can deal with problems ranging from very urgent requiring immediate action to longer term ones. Some therapy deals not with the immediate depressive problems but prevents relapse in the future.

Sometimes a pattern of responses to particular difficulties at home or work have become deranged, and the psychiatrist can give advice as to how to tackle them better in the future. For example: a wife overspends and gets into financial difficulty; or a husband constantly molests his teenage daughter. Often an accumulation of various personal, sexual, social and work difficulties together cause depression, and thoughts of suicide emerge because this appears to be the only way out.

All these problems can be unravelled. I have seen the most surprising and unexpected changes in some people where I felt, as they did, that there was absolutely no hope.

The Samaritans

Those in the religious professions have considerable practice in caring for people with suicidal feelings; it was a priest, Chad Varah, who started the Samaritans, the best known and, rightly, most respected agency for helping the suicidal and others in need.

The creation of the Samaritans in 1953 proved to be one of the most important developments in suicide prevention. It grew from small beginnings out of the Rev. Chad Varah's many years of experience of work in his City of London parish, St Stephen's Walbrook, still the home of the central London branch. He had seen the value of counselling and set up an organization to make it more generally available. A similar approach is now used worldwide. There are suicide prevention centres in the United States and elsewhere. In most the important feature is the 24-hour phone line coupled with counselling facilities and help of various kinds.

Following the setting up of the Samaritans the United Kingdom, in contrast to all other European countries, had a falling suicide rate; this pattern occurred wherever the Samaritans or similar voluntary organizations were introduced.

A book published by the Samaritans some years ago listed branches in over 40 countries, from Australia to Zimbabwe, offering a telephone line 24 hours a day for immediate help and advice. Numbers can be found in local telephone directories, public places or newspapers.

The watchword of the Samaritans is 'befriending'. This means responding to a suicidal person as a friend on an equal level, treating that person exactly as we ourselves would want to be treated in a crisis—with unconventional, uncritical acceptance and respect. After listening, help is made available and, most important, anything said is treated with complete confidentiality. The Samaritans see this as the answer to the person who feels rejected and vulnerable, that no-one cares and life is not worth living. 'I want to be dead' is often what the caller on the end of the phone says while the befriender's voice, manner and attitude attempts to counteract all these and many other negative feelings.

Many of the befrienders have themselves been 'rescued' by the Samaritans and therefore have a particular feeling for the problems. The Samaritans are quite clear that what they put forward is a therapeutic, not a social relationship and an offer of simple uncomplicated support. At times the befrienders may themselves find their task tedious and thankless, and it is true that many of the people who ring are very disturbed, tearful, aggressive, difficult, drunk or drugged. Some feel that they can take the Samaritans 'for a ride'. But the Samaritans are well aware of the difficulties they are likely to encounter and are alert to people who ring when there is other than a genuine need for help.

Other self-help organizations

In a crisis the individual usually turns to family, friends, acquaintances, the doctor or the priest. But if this seems inappropriate for various reasons there are other ways of seeking aid. Apart from the Samaritans, there are Befrienders International, or similar organizations world-wide.

Some local organizations deal only with minority groups; for example, I noticed a helpline advertized specifically for English ex-patriots in a holiday area of Spain! Radio stations and universities or polytechnics have helplines, and local hospital casualty departments or the police can give assistance depending on the need.

However, if the problem is less immediate, and maybe a family member as well as the individual needs help with an alcohol or drug problem, sexual difficulty or depression resulting from a recent bereavement, there are agencies that can help.

For many years groups of patients have set up self-help organizations, for example those for diabetes, and epilepsy; recently there has been a great expansion of these organizations all over the world. Many relate to all types of medical and psychiatric illness. To give an idea of the extent at both national and local level in the United Kingdom a 700-page directory was recently published. There are similar listings in many countries large and small, covering such problems as:

Addiction:	Alcohol, drugs, gambling.
Counselling:	Bereavement, divorce, sexual.
Disability:	Medical and mental handicaps.

These organizations are usually funded either by government grants or charitable appeals. They are staffed by those who have suffered similarly, backed by medical and other professionals such as social workers and counsellors. They fulfil a real need, both practical and social. The assistance offered is often immediate if for various reasons the usual medical or psychiatric services are unable to provide help.

These groups have helped many over the years with their advice, supplies of literature, provision of educational courses as well as informal group counselling. There is also evidence that apart from individuals and families receiving comfort suicide rates have fallen as a result.

If there is a real problem don't deny it; *seek help*.

Isolation and suicide

How can family, friends, workmates, or even casual acquaintances, who recognize that there is a problem, obtain help? It may be that all the usual sources of aid have been exhausted. The person intent on suicide often says: 'They can't help me. They didn't do anything before and they won't help me now.' Such statements often mean the reverse of what they imply, and the person must be guided towards professional or voluntary sources of help, preferably with whom they have had no previous contact.

Someone trying to help must make the first phone call or appointment on behalf of a potential suicide—to the family doctor, the priest, the social worker, the Samaritans, local radio station 'helplines'—and the police have information about many of the neighbourhood services available. In any case they should be called if there is any likelihood of violence.

Helping the destitute

Sadly, there are an increasing number of people with no network of friends, family or associates. They have cut themselves off, moved to large anonymous city centres or have been disowned because of their irrational behaviour; they have lost their way, lost any self-esteem, lost all real pleasure or reward for action. They leave a trail of disaster created partly by themselves, but also by the structure of society that demands certain behaviour patterns. How can they be helped and prevented from a progressive downhill course, to almost certain death not by suicide or accident, but from total neglect?

If a doubtful future is contemplated by either the helper or the victim there may seem to be no possibility of hope, so clutch at the immediate problem, aim at the very short-term solution, using a theme like that of 'Alcoholics Anonymous'—'one day at a time'. Survival for a few hours may bring success for another day, another week. It is surprising how very often a crisis passes. A few small crumbs can make a feast. Even in the blackest mood, everyone can 'get a lift' in the right environment, and a short breathing space is a success in itself.

Run through a checklist of possible agencies. Can any of them provide even one night in a hostel, or a meal? Is withdrawal from drugs for even a period all that is required now, or a hospital bed or a phone call to a long-lost friend?

Whatever the aims, what is needed initially is just a short

respite from troubles. We must not take on the impossible. Someone dying from cancer will die, but it need not be tonight. There may still be perhaps a few months or even a year of life left, which might give them some kind of happiness or peace, in a hospice, for example. This is an excellent alternative to a miserable death from a drug overdose, an end that will bring untold misery to the family, who have struggled and tried so hard to help.

We must be positive in our actions to help. Suicide is a response to a crisis for the individual, and as Professor Stengel, the foremost expert on suicide says, in his experience almost every suicide *could have been prevented.*

12

Conclusion: Hope for the Future

Suicide, then, is a problem as old as man himself, still with us and with increasing complexity as changes in life patterns come about even more speedily. This leads to changes in patterns of suicide, so everyone must be aware because it is all around us. Should the suicide of a loved one take place in spite of everything, I hope this book will help you to cope better, as well as assist others, who have to survive the tragedy and grief. In this final chapter I would like to consider all that has been written so far and underline a few important points.

First of all, even if you feel in utter despair, desperate, life is full of gloom, a tunnel of endless blackness, you must seek help. Don't forget that help is obtainable anonymously on the telephone via the Samaritans.

If someone in your family, friend or acquaintance is obviously in mental pain, it is important to assess the risk of suicide. It is usually high when a number of 'knocks' come together: death of a family member or close friend, serious illness, financial difficulty, redundancy or other similar life events. Perhaps the person is drinking heavily or taking tranquillizers in an effort to control their pain, which of course makes matters worse. Talk to them, persuade them to seek help, preferably outside the immediate circle of family and friends—doctor, priest, social worker, or counsellor (see Chapter 11). Bear in mind, though, that often those who commit suicide have been under the care of professionals in the preceding three months, and the contact has lapsed.

If things go badly wrong and you do have to cope with a suicide, it is best to be quite frank with everyone. Do not hide it; this 'bottling up' of the complex emotions that surround such a death can only make matters worse.

The numbness and despair just after a suicide changes quite quickly to feelings of guilt and anger. The 'if onlys' come thick and fast—I should have telephoned, written, visited etc—but do not forget that there is often a kind of inevitability to the event glimpsed at before and obvious afterwards. In many cases only a 24-hour guard under lock and key would prevent suicide. Sometimes this may be appropriate but we cannot necessarily predict with any accuracy the depth of the drive towards death or indeed the timing. Your only consolation is that at least you tried your best *in the circumstances*.

As time passes acceptance comes, the person is seen as a whole. The happy memories of a summer holiday, an outrageous game of poker, the funny fancy dress party, the friendship, the loving and tender moments. Time, though a healer, is slow and help may be needed in the resolution of the anger and guilt to allow a more peaceful view of the situation.

And finally, dare I reiterate that old adage: 'An ounce of prevention is worth a pound of cure'. I hope readers now have a greater ability to spot the warning signs that herald suicidal behaviour at home, school, work, indeed in any situation. I hope too they have a better idea of what action to take. If the worst happens, and it seems that the effect will never pass, all I can say is that it will. Not overnight, of course: it may be months or even years before a suicide is seen in perspective. Even if at the time one feels utterly despairing take comfort from the fact that there is help at hand. Though at times it seems extremely dim and distant, there is *always* a light at the end of the tunnel, as I know from my own experience.

Useful Addresses

It is difficult to give an accurate and up-to-date list because the network of help facilities changes frequently. Many have been set up over the past few years country-wide and are listed in local telephone directories, often with the emergency numbers for Police, Fire etc.

In the first instance a general practitioner, a previously-known social worker or counsellor or a local hospital should be consulted by the person seeking help or by a relative or friend on their behalf.

Here are a selection of the addresses of some important help facilities:

The Albany Trust
42 Chester Street, London SW1W 9HS. Tel 01-730 5871.
Personal counselling for those with sexual identity or relationship problems.

Alcoholics Anonymous
Addresses and phone numbers in local phone books, usually with emergency numbers. General Service Office UK, PO Box 1, Stonebow House, York YO1 2NJ. Tel 0904-644026.
Help for anyone with an honest desire to stop drinking.

Al-Anon
61 Great Dover Street, London SE1 4YF. Tel 01-403 0888.
Offers help to the families of problem drinkers.

British Association for Counselling
37a Sheep Street, Rugby, Warwickshire, CV21 3BX. Tel 0788-78328/9.
Promotes education and training for those involved in counselling.

Counselling for Young People
Tavistock Clinic, 12 Belsize Lane, NW3.

CRUSE
Cruse House, 126 Sheen Road, Richmond, Surrey, TW9 1VR. Tel 01-940 4818.
A service of counselling, advice and opportunities for social contact to all bereaved people.

Gingerbread
35 Wellington Street, London WC2E 7BN. Tel 01-240 0953.
A national network of local mutual aid groups providing emotional support, practical help and social activities for one-parent families.

MIND (*National Association of Mental Health*)
22 Harley Street, London W1N 2ED. Tel 01-637 0741.
Many activities to promote mental health and help the mentally disordered, including an information and advice service.

Psychiatric Emergencies
Many large hospitals offer emergency or crisis intervention services, for example The Maudsley Hospital, Denmark Hill, London SE5.

Relate (formerly the Marriage Guidance Council)
Addresses and phone numbers in local phone books.
London office: 76a New Cavendish Street, London W1.
Tel 01-580 1087.

Samaritans
17 Uxbridge Road, Slough, Berks SL1 1SN. Tel 0753-32713. Many local branches throughout the UK: see local phone book for details.
A 24-hour, absolutely confidential service for people who are in despair.

Terrence Higgins Trust
BM Aids London, WC1N 3XX. Tel 01-831 0330; helpline 01-242 1010.
Provides counselling, welfare and legal help for people with AIDS and their friends and families.

TRANX
National Tranquillizer Advice Centre, 25a Masons Avenue, Wealdstone, Harrow, Middx HA3 5AH.
Information and support for people suffering physical and psychological withdrawal symptoms from minor tranquillizers.

The Voluntary Euthanasia Society
13 Prince of Wales Terrace, London W8 5PG. Tel 01-937 7770.
Campaigns for a change in the law to allow voluntary euthanasia.

References and Further Reading

A book of this kind cannot be written without reference to other books on the subject. The following I mention specifically because of their value, and the fact that they may be useful to the reader wishing to follow up the subject.

Alvarez, A. *The Savage God: a study of suicide*. Penguin 1964.

Answers to Suicide, Presented to Chad Varah by the Samaritans on the twenty-fifth anniversary of their foundation. Constable 1987.

Baechler, Jean, tr. Cooper, Barry *Suicides*. Blackwell 1980.

Coleman, Vernon *Overcoming Stress*. Sheldon 1988.

Durkheim, Emile, tr. J. A. Spaulding and G. Simpson *Suicide*. Routledge and Kegan Paul 1952.

Hinton, John *Dying*. Penguin 1986.

Kubler-Ross, Elizabeth *On Death and Dying*. Tavistock Publications 1973.

Lake, Tony *Living with Grief*. Sheldon 1984.

Mental Health Foundation *Someone to Talk To*. Routledge and Kegan Paul 1985.

Parks, C. M. *Bereavement*. Penguin 1981.

REFERENCES

Stengel, E. *Suicide and Attempted Suicide*. Penguin 1964.

Roy, A., ed., *Suicide*. Baltimore, Williams and Wilkins, 1986.

Varah, Chad *The Samaritans – Befriending the Suicidal*. Constable 1980.

Index